Kaleidoscopic Grace

Ellie Emm Entry

Kaleidoscopic Grace © 2023 Ellie Emm Entry

Presentation by *BookLeaf Publishing*

Web: www.bookleafpub.com

E-mail: info@bookleafpub.com

ISBN: 9789357213349

First edition 2023

Dedicated to my mother and best friend,
Patricia Jane Terry,
to the promise I made that I intend to keep, to my
precious sparks, to my twice-in-a-lifetime Charming,
and to my dad for teaching me that giving up is not
an option.

You inspire me.

With special thanks to my Lord and Savior,
Jesus Christ, for taking all of the broken pieces,
making me whole again, and giving me a life worth
sharing.

(2 Corinthians 12:9)

somewhere in time

and although you are miles away

even the timeworn trees–

they whisper your name

carrying your breath across the wind

to surround me with your love

until we meet again

how do you want to be loved?

I don't need the flush of a constant spark.
I want to be loved at a passionate simmer
like the forest after it rains–

the way the earth drinks from its own roots,
tasting of the same sky it has been kissing
since the dawn of itself–
still enamored by its circular vitality.

Timeless.
  Vulnerable–
    yet somehow protected by everything it means.

        Atmospheric.

I want to be loved freely...
like etherean wings fresh out of their cocoon
delicately discovering themselves for the first time

            ...with promise.

2

I want to be loved with the poise
found in the strength of a martyr's last words.
Resonance with purpose.

I want to be loved with acquittal...
recklessly unabandoned
like the laws of maritime tradition;

the only way I know how–
the depths of which
cannot fathom
anything short of total surrender.

tiptoe

Tiptoe lightly across my mind;
even the slightest hint
of your presence reverberates–
an avalanching cascade
doused in your reflection.

Tread softly through my dreams;
for the footprints you make
remain unscathed–
even when other memories fade,
you're always there.

giovanni

Be wary of the limelight
Enjoy it while you're able
You're just a moment's whisper
Another fleeting tale

So expedite your curtsy
The next performer awaits
Scurry back behind the curtain
While the new muse takes your place

Don't wash off all your makeup
The opera isn't through
After intermission
The spotlight returns to you

Choose your aria wisely
You've only got one chance
Let Don Juan learn his lesson
Foolish cavorter of romance

Now stand up proudly, head held high
You've conquered tribulation
The final act was yours alone
So delight in your ovation.

postal

I seem to have misplaced my smile.
It used to live right on my face.
But today when I looked in the mirror,
I noticed it gone without trace.

I think that it went off to find you;
your affection it wanted to render.
If you discover you're no longer smitten,
simply mark, *"please return to sender."*

troy

In the guise of love,
you reached me
despite the stronghold
of these walls
to take advantage
of my weakness
and incite chaos
within my soul.

I'm battered
but still standing
as you carry on your way–
left breathing in the ashes
from the wreckage that remains.

drought season

You abandoned the oasis
for a puddle
and wonder why
the horizon
never brings any rain.

reverberation

This year, I resolve to be more acoustic...
to work hard to resonate with others instead of
effortlessly making noise...
to use my voice for harmony instead of rebuke.

This year, I resolve to be more acoustic...
to be amplified by time with loved ones instead of
shackled by jolts of electricity and digital tension...
defined by an echo.

This year, I resolve to be more acoustic...
to stand by my roots instead of on top of a
pedestal...
to project sincerity into a world so wantonly
synthesized.

This year, I resolve to be more acoustic...
to be true to my own composition—not
discounting the value of each measure
...imperfections and all.

This year, I resolve to be more acoustic...
to appreciate those who pause long enough in the
midst of their own crescendo

                        to listen to another's song.

analog

analog in a sundial world
where souls are traded for temporary bliss
catching light beams chased by shadows
with second hands grasping at the vitality
of moments taken for granted
by a society that doesn't notice
the countdown of a digital age
tick-tocking away
and 'watching your six'
only happens
for two minutes a day

subtleties

how foolish it is
to measure time
in heartbeats
instead of kisses
and love
with words
instead of diction

eleven eleven

Gazing deeply into the static pools of your soul
Tossing pennies–making wishes upon the stars that
they hold
Heads or tails?–Call your guess in the air
Mind over 'matter'–Will I find your love there?

Douse the candles all at once or in succession
But first, hold your hopes and answer this one
question

Why save your wishes for a single minute
when every heartbeat has magic in it?

haze

afraid of connection
in this cursory age
where forevers are temporary
and upgrades are praised

generationally instructed
to 'pass the buck' to all else
responsibility adjourned
in keeping the change to ourselves

passions turned lust
and obsession, without care
with "contact" defined
by 'likes', follows, and shares

double-tap to show 'love'
swipe left to throw shade–
no wonder we're living
in a world easily swayed

tea

you're *lavender*
when I'm seeking peace
chamomile
when I find it hard to sleep

kava
when my life feels like falling apart
green
when I could use that extra spark

you're *chai*
when life becomes too bland–
I hope with this,
you'll understand

that you're
my perfect cup of tea
and *honey*,
you're everything I need

mulligan

when I look at you,
I am regretful of the past–
of the things I would change,
given one more chance

when I look at you,
I am thankful for now;
there's a lot more to love,
but you're showing me how

when I look at you,
I watch our future unfold–
we've been through so much,
yet there's much left to behold

to cut to the chase–
it's you I've wanted so long;
no matter what's been,
you're my favorite love song

nocturnal serenade

Windsong *whispers* through the trees
Thunder rumbles *rhythmic beats*
Raindrops falling, *soothing breaths*
Such a *harmoniously melodic rest*

Lightning *crashes*, willows *sway*
Clouds come rolling, *nocturnal serenade*
Fantasy *beckons*, so I close my eyes
Thankful for Heaven's *acoustic lullaby*

confidential

You said you were an open book–
and with that, you did not lie;
you kept your pages visible
but redacted every line.

restoration

I was enamored by the intensity of summer
the sun beaming with the warmth of a thousand
smiles
all pointed towards me–
the heavens showing pride in my existence
You belong.

I was captivated by the perplexity of winter
the breeze caressing my skin like arms wrapped
tenderly
to shelter me from the frost–
careful exhales trembling my resolve
You are perennial.

I was fascinated by the provocation of spring
the freedom of wildflower abandon
twirling in the atmosphere–
fully aware of each rotation
You, too, will flourish.

I was smitten by the timeless vitality of autumn
the affirmation that change horizes—and it's
remarkable
sacrifice melting into rebirth
the inevitability of continuance amidst disruption
Your time is significant.

> *I fell in love with life*
> *when I accepted mine as a gift*
> *instead of a sentence.*

encore

ours was a twice-in-a-lifetime kind of love—
a wish come true
   even before the flight of the shooting star
     that would claim it through a child's eyes—
   and it was ours for the taking
both in unadulterated innocence
 and the wisdom of hindsight:
    past, present, and foreseeable future—
                 here we go again
the kind of passion that makes the heavens blush
  and mountains tremble beneath the gravity
    of shadows diminished
        by the brilliance of rebirth
as if the universe granted an echo to fate
    long enough to bring us back an encore

{he asked if it's too soon, or just long overdue...
        I say, at last, we're precisely on time.}

flamethrower

Precious spark,
you move like a whisper,
but it's okay to be loud.

Let your voice be saturated
by the confidence of your stride–
knowing that words alone
can ignite the exhale
and the only fuel you need
comes from within.

baggage claim

Do I really want to carry you into the new year
To make you my last and first kiss
The past ones were ridden with heartache
And you're largely to blame for all this

Do I really want to carry you into the new year
And struggle with the burdens you've bestowed
Fighting your demons off one by one
When I've got plenty enough of my own

Do I really want to carry you into the new year
Along with the weight of your treason
Or should I lift the heaviness off my own heart
And forgive you for that very reason

Do I really want to carry you into the new year
And chance that you'll suddenly atone
For sins unrepented that I cannot judge
Between you and your Maker alone

Do I really want to carry you into the new year
Or is it time that I give up the fight
Leaving our baggage at the end of December
To start January traveling light

pinky promise

I see through the nightmares
and into your soul
the guilt that you feel
and lies you've been told

I know that you're hiding
from pasts you regret
so hold my hand tightly–
it's not over just yet

Your mind isn't broken
despite what some say;
so let's banish the monsters
and conquer the day

Printed in the USA
CPSIA information can be obtained
at www.ICGtesting.com
LVHW011356140724
785413LV00011B/585